Sloths as Pets

Sloths as Pets

The Complete Guide to Keeping a Sloth as a Pet

Including Two-Toed and Three-Toed

Facts on Sloths for Sale, Eating, Teeth, Habitat, Health, Endangered Status and Charities

Ladders of Success Ltd, West Wing, Framfield Place, TN22 5QH, United Kingdom

ISBN 978-1-905311-06-4

Disclaimer

Although the author and publisher have made every effort to ensure that the information in this book was correct at press time, the author and publisher do not assume and hereby disclaim any liability to any party for any loss, injury, damage or disruption caused by errors or omissions, whether such errors or omissions result from negligence, accident, non-functional websites, or any other cause. Any advice or strategy contained herein may not be suitable for every individual.

Foreword

The sloth is a unique and beautiful creature that has started to gain popularity as an exotic pet. What many people who want a sloth as a pet forget, however, is that sloths are wild animals. Not only is it difficult to legally obtain a sloth for a pet, but these animals require a great deal of specialized care. If you are considering the sloth as a pet you would do well to learn everything you can about them – that is where this book comes in.

In reading this book you will receive a wealth of information about the sloths including sloth facts, history, conservation, and more. You will also receive detailed information about keeping and feeding a sloth in captivity. By the time you finish this book you should have a deep understanding of the sloth and a better idea whether or not it is the right pet for you.

Acknowledgements

I would like to extend my sincerest thanks to my friends and family for supporting me as I wrote this book. Special thanks as well to all of those who donate to and support sloth conservation efforts.

Table of Contents

Chapter One: Introduction..1

Important Terms to Know 3

Chapter Two: Understanding the Sloth.........................6

1) What Are Sloths?..7

2) Facts About the Sloth...9

Summary of Sloth Facts.....................................12

3) Conservation Efforts...14

4) Sloth Species 16

5) Evolutionary History of Sloths 29

6) Cautions of Owning a Sloth 31

Chapter Three: What to Know Before You Buy...................33

1) Do You Need a License? 34

a) CITES Protection of Sloths............................35

b) Owning a Sloth Legally.................................36

2) How Many Should You Buy?..............................38

3) Can Sloths Be Kept with Other Pets? 39

4) Ease and Cost of Care......................................40

a) Initial Costs 40

b) Monthly Costs 43

5) Pros and Cons of the Sloth...............................46

Chapter Four: Caring for the Sloth 48

1) Habitat Requirements 49

2) Accessorizing Your Sloth Cage 52

3) Sloth Cage Maintenance 54

Chapter Five: Feeding Your Sloth 56

1) Sloth Nutritional Needs 57

2. Sample Diets in Captivity 60

Chapter Six: Breeding Sloths 65

1) Sloth Breeding Info 66

Chapter Seven: Keeping Your Sloth Healthy 69

1) Common Health Problems 70

2) Preventing Illness in Sloths 76

a) Dealing with Nutritional Deficiencies 77

b) Maintaining Sanitary Conditions 78

3) Medical Benefits of Fungus in Sloth Fur 79

Chapter Eight: Sloth Care Sheet 81

1) Basic Information 82

2) Habitat Set-up Guide 84

3) Nutritional Needs 85

4) Breeding Information 86

Chapter Nine: Relevant Websites 88

1) Food for Your Sloth 89

2) Cages and Cage Supplies for Sloth 90

3) Sloth Species Information 92

4) Conservation Information for Sloths 94

Chapter Ten: Frequently Asked Questions 95

Index...100

Photo Credits 109

References...113

Chapter One: Introduction

The sloth is a jungle-dwelling mammal known for its slow movements and long, curved claws that help it grasp tree branches high up in the canopy. These animals are native to parts of Central and South America and they generally live their lives up in the trees, although there are several extinct species of aquatic sloth. The sloth is a wild animal, but it has recently begun to gain popularity as an exotic pet. For the qualified and educated owner, a sloth can make an interesting pet – however, it is by no means easy to care for. Owning a sloth as a pet is not the right choice for everyone and, even if you decide that it is, you won't have an easy time finding one legally.

If you are thinking about keeping a sloth as a pet it is imperative that you learn everything you can about these beautiful animals. There are two main types of sloths – two-toed and three-toed - some of which are considered "Critically Endangered" by the IUCN. Keeping a sloth as a pet is not something that should be taken lightly, even if you were able to obtain one legally. Before you decide that a sloth is the right pet for you, you need to learn the proper way to care for these animals in captivity to assure that your new pet remains happy and healthy.

In this book you will learn everything you need to know in order to decide whether the sloth is the right pet for you. In addition to learning basic facts about these animals, you will also receive specific tips and information about creating the ideal sloth habitat and crafting a special diet for your sloth. By the time you finish reading this book, you will have a deeper understanding of the sloth in general as well as the conservation issues related to the species. You will also learn the pros and cons of keeping a sloth as a pet. If, after reading all of this information, you still believe that the sloth is the right pet for you then you will be well on your way to becoming the best sloth owner you can be.

So, if you are ready to start learning about the sloth, then turn the page and keep reading!

Important Terms to Know

Arboreal – Referring to an animal that lives almost exclusively in the trees.

Carnivore – An animal that subsists mainly on meat.

CITES - The Convention on International Trade in Endangered Species of Wild Fauna and Flora; a multilateral treaty that protects endangered wildlife from international trade and sale.

Conception – Fertilization resulting in pregnancy.

Conservation – The act of preserving, guarding or protecting; generally refers to a species or natural resource.

Defense Mechanism – A coping technique animals develop to protect themselves from predators

Dioiecious – Meaning that a species has distinct male and female organisms.

Folivore – A type of herbivore that feeds primarily on leaves; have anatomical adaptations to digest leaves.

Gestation Period – The period of time during which a baby sloth develops in its mother's womb.

Gland - An organ that produces and secretes a certain substance.

Herbivore – An animal that subsists almost exclusively on plant matter.

Nocturnal – An animal that is more active at night rather than during the day; like the two-toed sloth.

Omnivore – An animal that subsists on both plant matter and meat for food.

Primary Forest - A forest that has reached mature condition by being undisturbed for a long time.

Polygynandrous - A type of sexual relationship in which two or more males have exclusive relationships with two or more females.

Secondary Forest - A forest that has re-grown following a major disturbance such as fire or harvest; has not yet reached a mature state.

Sexual Dimorphism – Physical differences between males and females of the same species.

Terrestrial – Referring to an animal that lives on the ground (rather than in the trees).

Vestigial - An organ or structure that has diminished in size through evolution to the point where it is no longer functional.

Chapter Two: Understanding the Sloth

Even before opening this book you probably already know the basics about sloths. Sloths are slow-moving animals that live in the trees, spending much of their life hanging upside down. Though these things are true, there is so much more to learn about these animals – especially if you are thinking about keeping one as a pet. In this chapter you will receive a wealth of information about sloths in general as well as information about each species to help you get a better understanding of sloths. You will also receive some cautionary information about keeping sloths as pets as well as important conservation information.

1) *What Are Sloths?*

The sloth is a medium-sized mammal that lives primarily in the trees, making it an arboreal animal. Sloths belong to one of two taxonomical families – Megalonychidae and Bradypodidae. Between these two families there are six different species of sloth. Sloths are related to anteaters because they belong to the same taxonomical order, Pilosa, and they have a similarly specialized set of claws. While the anteater uses its claws to dig up termite nests, the sloth uses its claws to climb high up in the canopy.

Sloths are either two-toed or three-toed and the name "sloth" is derived from the Latin and Greek words for "leaf-eater". These animals are classified as folivores which means that the majority of their diet consists of tender shoots, buds and leaves. While sloths will feed to some degree on any kind of tree, most of their food comes from Cecropia trees, a genus of trees found in the Neotropical regions of the world. In addition to vegetation, some sloths have been documented eating other foods including insects and small reptiles – even birds.

What makes the sloth interesting, aside from its slow movement, is the fact that it has many very specialized adaptations. In addition to its long, curved claws the sloth also has specialized fur which grows in the opposite direction you would expect from most mammals. In most mammals, fur grows toward the extremities. For the sloth, however, the fur grow in the opposite direction because this animal spends so much of its time with its arms and legs raised above its body. The opposite direction of hair growth helps to protect the sloth from the elements while it is hanging upside down.

In addition to growing in the opposite direction of most mammals, the sloth's fur is also home to a small ecosystem in and of itself. In the sloth's fur you will find two different species of symbiotic algae which help to provide the sloth with camouflage. This is very important because the sloth moves very slowly so it is unlikely to outrun a predator – its slow movement also acts as a form of self-defense since it does not attract much attention with its movements. You will also find a number of different non-parasitic insects in the sloth's coat that feed on those two types of algae. Some of the insects most likely to inhabit a sloth's coat include moths, beetles, and cockroaches.

2) *Facts About the Sloth*

Though the details vary among the different species, the sloth is generally about the size of a medium-sized dog. Two-toed sloths are typically a little larger than three-toed sloths, weighing between 9 and 17 lbs. (4 to 8kg) and measuring 23 to 27.5 inches (58 to 70 cm) long. The three-toed sloth generally weighs between 8 and 10 lbs. (3.5 to 4.5 kg) and measures up to 18 inches (45cm) long. The three-toed sloth has a short tail and three clawed toes on each of its limbs. The two-toed sloth has two clawed toes on its front limbs and three on its hind limbs. Two-toed sloths also exhibit longer fur and a more prominent snout than three-toed sloths.

Another interesting anatomical feature of the sloth is its vertebrae. The three-toed sloth is very unusual among mammals because it possesses up to nine cervical vertebrae, compared to the average of seven. The toe-toed sloth and the manatee are the only other mammals to have this kind of spine formation. In terms of its dentition, the sloth has no incisors or true canine teeth. The sloth has one canine-like tooth called a caniniform which is separated from the other teeth which are called molariforms. The molariforms are used to grind food – this is how the sloth expends the majority of its energy.

Sloths move an average of about 40 yards per day, eating vegetation as they go along. The sloth's average rate of speed is only about 0.15 mph (0.24 km/h) and they move between different trees about three or four times a day. The sloth uses its arms and legs to move along tree branches but on the ground they do not move very well – they have to use their claws to pull their bodies along. The sloth is an agile swimmer, however, and they sometimes drop into the water from their perches in the trees.

The sloth is primarily known for its slow movement, but its physical movement is not the only thing about it that is slow. These animals have very slow-acting stomachs as well – it is an adaptation to their vegetation-heavy diet. The leaves the sloth eats provide little in the way of nutrients and energy, plus they are very difficult to digest. So, the sloth developed a very specialized stomach with multiple compartments. The stomach is full of symbiotic bacteria which help to break down the leaves so the sloth can digest them and extract the nutrients. The digestive process for a sloth can take as long as a month (or more) to be fully completed.

In addition to having a very slow-moving digestive system, the sloth also has a very slow metabolism. The metabolic rate of a sloth is less than half the rate of other mammals its size. The sloth has an average body temperature as low as

86°F to 93°F (30°C to 34°C) while it is active and it drops even lower when the sloth is resting. This slow metabolic rate is another adaptation related to the fact that the sloth's diet provides very little energy.

Because the sloth moves very slowly it doesn't attract much attention – this is an important defense mechanism. The only method the sloth has for self-defense is its claws. When cornered, a sloth might swipe at its attackers with its long, curved claws either in hopes of wounding the predator or scaring it away. It is a fairly rare occasion, however, for a sloth to be attacked by a predator when it is up in the trees. Sloths become most vulnerable when they are on the ground. In fact, the sloth only has three main predators – jaguars, harpy eagles, and humans.

The only times a sloth will come down from the trees is to urinate and defecate. They do this about once a week, digging a hole and then covering it up afterwards. Sloths generally go to the same spot each time and they are at high risk for predation as they do so. It is unknown why the sloth goes to ground level to relieve itself, but it may be because defecating from high in the trees might produce noise that would attract predators. It is also possible that the smell from these holes is what sloths use to find each other for breeding purposes. The sloth has a very weak sense of hearing and their eyesight is not strong, so they rely heavily on their sense of smell.

Female sloths generally give birth to one baby each year, though sometimes it will take a female more than a year to find a . After being born, the baby sloth will cling to its mothers' fur. If the baby falls off it generally survives the fall but it may die from exposure or starvation because the mother may be unwilling to leave the safety of the trees to retrieve it. In terms of sexual dimorphism, male and female sloths are not highly differentiated. In fact, it is not uncommon for zoos to purchase sloths of the wrong sex. Sloths reach sexual maturity around 3 to 5 years of age and they have a lifespan around 20 to 30 years.

Summary of Sloth Facts

Taxonomy: order Pilosa; family Megalonychidae or Bradypodidae

Species: six species currently identified

Distribution: Central and South America

Habitat: almost entirely arboreal

Size: varies by species, generally 19 to 27 inches (50 to 70cm) long; weigh between 17.5 and 18.75 lbs. (about 8kg)

Body Shape: long arms and legs; short head with large eyes, short snouts and tiny ears; stubby tails; long, curved claws; long tongues

Fur Length: longer in two-toed sloths

Tail: absent in two-toed sloths; 2.4 to 2.75 inches (6 to 7cm) in three-toed sloths

Coloration: varies from one species to another; primarily shades of brown and tan; camouflaged with algae growth

Movement: primarily suspension-based and quadrupedal; very slow and deliberate

Defense Mechanisms: slow movement (doesn't disturb surrounding vegetation); long, sharp claws

Diet: folivore; primarily feeds on tender shoots, buds, and leaves; occasionally eat insects, small reptiles, and birds

Adaptations: multi-compartment stomach filled with symbiotic bacteria; bacteria helps to break down leaves

Metabolism: very slow metabolic rate, half the rate of similar-sized mammals; body temperature as low as 86°F to 93°F (30°C to 34°C) while active

Gestation Period: about 6 to 11 months, varies by species

Infants: born upside down; cling to mother's fur for several weeks then may continue to follow her for up to 4 years

Lifespan: average 20 to 30 years in the wild, often longer in captivity

3) Conservation Efforts

In its native habitat, the sloth plays a very important role in the ecosystem. Not only does it support the growth of algae, bacteria, and various insects in its fur but its habit of defecating in holes they dig in the ground helps to fertilize the substrate for the growth of vegetation. Unfortunately, because the sloth is almost entirely arboreal, it is heavily affected by deforestation – poaching is also a serious problem for sloths.

According to the IUCN Red List, four of the six sloth species are labeled "Least Concern" in terms of conservation. The Maned Sloth (*Bradypus torquatus*) is listed as "Vulnerable" and the Pygmy Three-Toed Sloth (*Bradypus Pygmaeus*) is "Critically Endangered". There are a number of conservation groups which are working to conserve the various sloth species. The World Wildlife Fund (WWF) works together with local communities, governments and companies to encourage sustainable forestry methods.

The Sloth Sanctuary in Costa Rica is dedicated to rescuing and preserving sloths. The sanctuary has rescued over 500 sloths since its founding in 1997 and they have rehabilitated and released more than 120 sloths. Today the sanctuary offers tours and educational programs – they also work with researchers to improve the world's understanding of the sloth.

If you want to do your part in supporting conservation efforts for the sloth, visit some of the links below:

Sloth Sanctuary of Costa Rica.

<http://www.slothsanctuary.com/>

Sloth – World Wildlife Fund.

<http://www.worldwildlife.org/species/sloth>

Slothville – The Sloth Appreciation Society.

<http://www.slothville.com/about-slothville/#.VmXxJ_ mrQuU>

Save Our Sloths – IndieGoGo Campaign.

<https://www.indiegogo.com/projects/save-our-sloths#/>

4) Sloth Species

Now that you know the basics about sloths in general you may be curious to learn the details about each of the six different species. In this section you will receive an overview of each sloth species. <u>The six sloth species which have been identified as distinct species include</u>:

- Pale-Throated Sloth (*Bradypus tridactylus*)
- Brown-Throated Sloth (*Bradypus variegatus*)
- Maned Sloth (*Bradypus torquatus*)
- Pygmy Three-Toed Sloth (*Bradypus pygmaeus*)
- Hoffman's Two-Toed Sloth (*Choloepus hoffmanni*)
- Linnaeus' Two-Toed Sloth (*Choloepus didactylus*)

Pale-Throated Sloth (*Bradypus tridactylus*)

The pale-throated sloth is a variety of three-toed sloth and it is found throughout the northern region of South America. This species is frequently confused with the brown-throated sloth but it is more widely distributed and they have a pale yellow patch of color on the throat. The pale-throated sloth has a rounded head and blunt nose with two very small, external ears. This species has long limbs like any sloth but they are fairly weak – the sloth relies on its long, curved claws to propel itself through the trees.

Males of the pale-throated sloth species grow up to 18 to 22 inches in body length and they have a short stubby tail measuring 1.6 to 2.4 inches (4 to 6 cm). Females are actually significantly larger than males, measuring 20 to 30 inches (50 to 75 cm) in length and weighing up to 14.3 lbs. (6.5 kg) – this is in comparison to the average weight of 7 to 13 lbs. (3 to 6 kg) for males.

What sets the pale-throated sloth apart from other species is its long fur. The body of this sloth is covered in coarse guard hairs that grow up to 4 inches (10 cm) long – these hairs grow over a fine undercoat. The pale-throated sloth has a blackish-gray coloring over its whole body with darker patches on the hips, shoulders, and back. In many cases, males also exhibit a bright orange or yellow patch of fur on the back which is divided down the middle by a black stripe. The coloration on the throat is pale yellow in color which helps to distinguish the species from the similar-looking brown-throated sloth.

Brown-Throated Sloth (*Bradypus variegatus*)

The brown-throated sloth is also a species of three-toed sloth and it is frequently confused with the pale-throated sloth. This species can be found throughout the neotropical ecozone in Central and South America. The brown-throated sloth is similar in size and build to other three-toed species so it is the brown coloration on its throat that sets it apart. This species grows to about 17 to 31 inches (42 to 80 cm) in body length for both males and females with the addition of a short tail measuring 1 to 3.5 inches (2.5 to 9 cm) long.

Adult brown-throated sloths weigh between 5 and 14 lbs. (2.25 to 6.3 kg) on average. Like most sloths, the brown-throated sloth has a rounded head and blunt nose with very small ears. This sloth exhibits a gray-brown coloration with a beige tint and they have darker brown fur on the throat (hence the name of the species). This species also has darker brown fur on the forehead and the sides of the face while the face itself is pale in color with a dark stripe running under the eyes.

The brown-throated sloth has a coat of stiff, coarse guard hairs over a soft, dense undercoat. As is true for all sloths, the coat is home to myriad species of algae and symbiotic bacteria as well as various insects. The brown-throated sloth travels slowly and parts of its range overlaps with that of the Hoffmann's two-toed sloth. In places where the two overlap, the brown-throated sloth is more active in general (even during the day) and more numerous in population. In fact, the brown-throated sloth is the most widely distributed and the most common of all of the three-toed sloth species.

Maned Sloth (*Bradypus torquatus*)

The maned sloth is another three-toed sloth but it is only found in Brazil. This species primarily inhabits the Atlantic coastal rainforest in the southeastern region of Brazil, though it was at one time found in some areas further to the north. The maned sloth lives largely in evergreen forest but because it can digest a variety of types of vegetation it is sometimes found in semi-deciduous forest as well. The main concern for this species is a hot, humid climate that lacks a dry season.

This species of sloth has a thick coat of coarse guard hairs over a short, dense undercoat. The undercoat is white and black in color while the outer coat ranges from pale brown to gray. As is true for all sloths, the outer coat plays host to a variety of algae and insects. The maned sloth earns its name, however, from the mane of black hair that runs down its neck and over the shoulders. This mane is usually thicker and darker in males – in females it may be reduced to a few long tufts of hair.

The adult male maned sloth measures between 22 and 28 inches (55 to 72 cm) long with a 2-inch (5 cm) tail. Females are significantly larger than males, measuring 22 to 30 inches (55 to 75 cm) long and weighing 10 to 22 lbs. (4.5 to 10 kg) compared to the male's 9 to 16.5 lbs. (4 to 7.5 kg). Compared to other mammals its size, the sloth has very little muscle mass so it relies on its curved claws to hold on to branches as it moves through the canopy. Maned sloths are largely diurnal, spending about 60% to 80% of their day sleeping and moving between tress for the remainder of their time.

Pygmy Three-Toed Sloth (*Bradypus Pygmaeus*)

Also known as the dwarf sloth or the monk sloth, the pygmy three-toed sloth is the smallest of the sloth species. This species is endemic to a small island off the coast of Panama known as Isla Escudo de Veraguas. This species of sloth was only described as recently as 2001 and it is thought to have diverged from the brown-throated sloth after the island was separated from the mainland about 8900 years ago.

The pygmy three-toed sloth is about 40% smaller in mass than other sloths, weighing only 5.5 to 7.7 lbs. (2.5 to 3.5 kg) – it is also about 15% smaller in length. This species measures between 19 and 21 inches (48 to 53 cm) in length at maturity and has a small tail measuring 1.8 to 2.4 inches (4.5 to 6 cm) in length. Pygmy three-toed sloths have tan-colored fur on the face with orange patches over the eyes and a dark brown band running across the brow. Most specimens exhibit blotchy coloration on the back, often with a dark brown stripe. What makes this species physically unique (aside from its size) is the long for on the sides and crown of the head that looks like a hood.

This species of three-toed sloth is an arboreal species, like all sloths. What makes it unique, however, is the fact that it is found only in red mangroves and it is able to digest the coarse leaves. Compared to the *Cecropia* trees where other sloths feed, red mangroves are a very poor source of nutrition. This species has only 18 teeth that it uses to grind the tough leaves – 10 teeth in the upper jaw and 8 in the lower. Two of the teeth in both the upper and lower jaw are incisor-like, though the incisor-like teeth may be smaller in the upper jaw.

Hoffman's Two-Toed Sloth (*Choloepus hoffmanni*)

The Hoffman's two-toed sloth is one of two two-toed species and it is found throughout Central and South America. This species is different from the three-toed species because it only has two clawed fingers on its front two limbs. Other anatomical differences between the two- and three-toed sloths include a longer snout, a larger size overall, and separate toes on the forefeet (the three-toed sloth's toes are partially fused).

The Hoffman's two-toed sloth is an arboreal species like all sloths but it is nocturnal. This species lives in the rainforest canopy and there are actually five recognized subspecies which include:

- *Choleopus hoffmani hoffmanni*
- *Choleopus hoffmani agustinus*
- *Choleopus hoffmani capitalis*
- *Choleopus hoffmani juruanus*
- *Choleopus hoffmani pallescens*

This species of sloth is larger than the three-toed sloth varieties, measuring about 21 to 28 inches (54 to 72 cm) in body length and weighing from 4.6 to 19.8 lbs. (2 to 9 kg). The Hoffmani two-toed sloth does have a stubby tail, but it is shorter than that of other sloths and is usually not visible through the fur. This species of sloth has tan to light brown fur with lighter coloring on the face. Females are generally larger than males, but there is a considerable amount of overlap in terms of size.

Linnaeus' Two-Toed Sloth (*Choloepus didactylus*)

The second of the two-toed sloth species is Linnaeus' two-toed sloth, also known as Linne's two-toed sloth or the southern two-toed sloth. This species is found throughout South America in parts of Colombia, Venezuela, Peru, Ecuador, and Brazil – generally in areas north of the Amazon River. This species is larger than most three-toed sloths and it has larger eyes, longer hair, and its front and back limbs are closer to equal in length.

Linnaeus' two-toed sloth measures about 18 to 34 inches (46 to 86 cm) in body length and it has a very short tail measuring 0.5 to 1.5 inches (1.5 to 3.5 cm) – the tail is so short that it is generally not visible through the long fur. This species weighs between 8.75 and 19 lbs. (4 to 8.5 kg) and it has long, coarse fur that comes in varying shades of brown or tan. Also noteworthy is the fact that this species has very few teeth, only four to five sets of teeth including the canines, and they have no incisors.

Like the Hoffmann's two-toed sloth, Linnaeus' two-toed sloth is also nocturnal. This species feeds primarily on fruits and leaves and its primary predators include birds of prey, ocelots, and humans. This species can swim, but it tends to travel primarily by tree where it can eat leaves as it goes along. When the sloth is in the water it has a higher risk of predation by large snakes like the anaconda.

5) Evolutionary History of Sloths

You have already learned that the sloth is a type of mammal belonging to the order Pilosa and that there are two families of sloth – Megalonychidae (two-toed sloths) and Bradypodidae (three-toed sloths). If you back things up a little further, you will find that sloths belong to the superorder Xenarthra which also contains anteaters and armadillos. This group of mammals developed in South America an estimated 60 million years ago. The earliest mammals belonging to this group are thought to have been arboreal herbivores, similar in anatomy to the modern sloth.

Although the name "two-toed sloth" would suggest otherwise, all modern sloths have three toes – that is, three toes on their hind limbs. The two-toed sloth species are so named because they have two fingers on their front limbs. These species occupy similar parts of the forest as three-toed sloths but they are able to move more quickly. Though two-toed and three-toed sloths exhibit a number of physical similarities, their taxonomical relationship is more distant than you might think. It is believed that the common ancestor of two-toed and three-toed sloths diverged approximately 35 to 40 million years ago. Modern sloth species, then, are excellent examples of parallel or convergent evolution.

Parallel evolution is a term used to describe the development of similar characteristics in related but distinctly separate species descended from a common ancestor. The evolutionary history of three-toed sloth species are poorly understood, but it is thought that modern two-toed sloths are more closely related to extinct species of ground sloth than to the modern three-toed sloth. It is unclear whether these ground sloths descended from arboreal ancestors or if modern two-toed sloths are simply miniature versions of the ground sloth that adapted to arboreal life.

6) Cautions of Owning a Sloth

The most important thing you need to remember when keeping a sloth as a pet is that the sloth is a wild animal – you may be able to tame a sloth to some degree, but it will never be completely domesticated. Like any animal, the sloth will not hesitate to defend itself if it feels threatened. Sloths have very long, sharp claws that can do some serious damage if you aren't careful – you may also be at risk for infection if you are scratched by a sloth and do not take care of the injury properly.

Another important factor to consider before choosing a sloth as a pet is the amount of time and effort that goes into caring for a sloth, not to mention the expense. The sloth follows a very specialized diet in the wild so you must be able to recreate that diet in order for your sloth to thrive. Keep in mind that different species of sloth have slightly different nutritional needs, so be sure to do your research before you choose a species. It is also essential that you provide your sloth with the right kind of habitat – sloths need to be able to climb in the trees because they are not adapted to walking on the ground.

One final thing to consider when you are thinking about owning a sloth is what you are going to do if the sloth gets sick. If you have a dog or a cat that gets sick you can simply take it to the veterinarian for a check-up. This is not the case with a sloth because most veterinarians are not trained to handle this kind of animal. You might be able to find an exotics vet but you may have to take your sloth to a zoo vet for treatment if he gets sick. Not only is it difficult to find a vet qualified to care for your sloth, but it will be expensive as well.

Chapter Three: What to Know Before You Buy

Before you decide whether or not the sloth is the right pet for you, you need to take the time to learn about the practical aspects of keeping and caring for these animals. Sloths are very different from traditional pets like cats and dogs – they will not thrive unless you take the time to learn about and provide for their needs. In this chapter you will learn about licensing requirements for sloths as well as tips for keeping sloths with other pets, estimated costs for keeping a sloth, and a list of pros and cons for these beautiful animals.

1) Do You Need a License?

If you are thinking about keeping a sloth as a pet, the first thing you need to consider is whether it is legal for you to do so. For one thing, many states and cities do not allow the keeping of exotic pets and those that do often have restrictions regarding the species you are allowed to keep. In addition to thinking about the legality of keeping a sloth in your area, you also have to determine whether you can obtain a sloth legally. According to Born Free USA, sloths are one of the hottest black market items in Colombia (aside from drugs and weapons). Plus, a 2012 Nightline report estimated that more than 60,000 exotic animals were illegally trafficked in Colombia alone – many of those exotic animals were sloths.

In the event that you are able to legally obtain a sloth, keep in mind that licensing and permit requirements may vary from one area to another. You need to be very sure that you understand the specific requirements for the area in which you live. In the following pages you will find tips for determining licensing requirements and for keeping the sloth as a pet legally.

a) CITES Protection of Sloths

Because the sloth is a wild animal (and an endangered species), your first concern in thinking about purchasing one of these animals is whether or not it is protected by federal law. The main form of protection sloths have comes from CITES – the Convention on International Trade in Endangered Species of Wild Fauna and Flora. This multilateral treaty was originally put into force in 1975 and it has been regularly updated with new protected species every year.

The list of animals protected by CITES includes three appendices labeled I, II and III. Appendix I animals are those which are most endangered. Because these species are threatened with extinction, international trade of these animals is prohibited except when the purpose is not commercial (scientific research, for example). None of the six sloth species are listed under Appendix I but two species are listed under Appendix II (*Bradypus pygmaeus* and *Bradypus variegatus*) and one is listed under Appendix III (*Choloepus hoffmanni*).

Animals listed in Appendix II are not necessarily threatened with extinction currently but they may become threatened if trade is not closely controlled. For these species, international trade may be authorized with the granting of an export permit. An import permit is not necessary for these species under CITES, but some countries enforce stricter measures for import and export. Animals listed under CITES Appendix III are those which are already regulated but the help of other countries is required to prevent illegal exploitation. International trade of these species is only allowed in cases where the appropriate permits have been issued.

According to the Humane Society of the United States, there are only seven states that allow the keeping of exotic animals without a license. These states include Alabama, Nevada, North Carolina, Ohio, South Carolina, West Virginia, and Wisconsin. If you live in one of these states you will not face any legal restrictions for keeping a sloth as a pet but you must still find a way to obtain the sloth legally or face serious consequences.

b) Owning a Sloth Legally

When it comes to obtaining and owning a sloth legally as a pet, you really only have two options. One option is to apply for a permit that will allow you to keep an endangered species as a pet. Unless you are affiliated with a zoo or a rescue operation, this is extremely unlikely. Even if you do obtain the necessary permit you will still have difficulty finding a sloth that is legally available. If you purchase a sloth illegally you face the threat of prosecution if you are caught.

Your second option for obtaining and keeping a sloth is to find a country that does not adhere to the restrictions of CITES. If you are able to obtain a sloth from one of these countries, however, your only option to keep the animal is to move to that country. You will not be able to export a sloth without a permit and you are extremely unlikely to get one. Another option is to obtain a certification as a naturalist but you will still have to obtain the sloth legally and will be required to use it for educational purposes in order to keep it.

Note: If you love sloths, the best thing you can do is to not keep one. Sloths are wild animals and some species are critically endangered – supporting the illegal trade of these animals means contributing to their decline in the wild. If you do happen to come across a sloth for sale, consider reporting it to a rescue group rather than trying to purchase it and keep it yourself.

2) How Many Should You Buy?

Little is known about the social structure sloths follow in the wild but it is generally believed that these animals are fairly solitary. A baby sloth may cling to its mother's fur for several weeks until it is weaned but it may then stay with the mother for as long as four years. For the most part, however, sloths do not tend to live in social groups so it is not a requirement that you keep more than one sloth together. In fact, keeping two male sloths together could be dangerous because they might fight for territory. You also have to consider the difficulty level of obtaining and caring for these animals. Finding and caring for one sloth is a major task, so keeping two of them will be even more of a challenge for you.

3) Can Sloths Be Kept with Other Pets?

The sloth has not been documented interacting much with other animals in the wild and these animals are generally believed to be solitary in terms of their social structure. This being the case, it is not a good idea to keep a sloth with other pets. You also have to consider the fact that the sloth is a wild animal – there is a great deal of risk involved with keeping these animals along with other more traditional pets like cats and dogs.

If you visit your local zoo, you may see other animals being kept in the same habitat as a sloth – fruit bats are a popular example. In cases like this, the two species do not compete for food and they can generally go about their business without disturbing the other. In zoos, however, keeping multiple species in one enclosure is largely done to add to the viewing interest – it is generally not for the benefit of the animals in the enclosure. So think carefully before keeping any other animals with your sloth.

4) Ease and Cost of Care

The sloth is not a traditional pet so you shouldn't expect to spend the same amount on its care as you would for a dog or a cat. Not only is it much more difficult (and expensive) to purchase a sloth, but the cost of upkeep is much higher as well. If you are thinking about keeping a sloth as a pet you should take the time to consider the associated costs. If you cannot financially support your sloth, caring for all of his basic needs, you should choose another pet. In this section you will receive an overview of the costs associated with keeping a pet sloth.

a) Initial Costs

The initial cost associated with keeping sloths as pets include those costs which you must cover before bringing your sloth home and to purchase the animal. Initial costs include the purchase price of the sloth, the cost of the cage, necessary accessories and a lighting system. Below you will find a brief explanation of each initial cost as well as an estimate and total cost summary.

Purchase Price – One of the largest costs associated with pet sloths is, of course, the sloth itself. Setting aside the difficulty of actually finding a sloth for sale legally, consider that the purchase price for a sloth will range from about $1,500 to $3,000 (£1,350 - £2,700).

Cage – Because the sloth is not a traditional pet you cannot just go to the pet store and buy a sloth cage – you will probably have to build one on your own. Sloths are arboreal mammals so they need plenty of vines and branches to climb on – this may mean that you will have to build your sloth cage around a tree or construct a network of branches for climbing. Depending on the size of your cage and how detailed you want to get, the cost could range from a few hundred dollars to a few thousand. You should budget a cost of $500 to $2,000 (£450 - £1,800) for your sloth enclosure.

Cage Accessories/Supplies – Sloths are not the kind of pet that need a lot of toys in their cage but you should provide some opportunities for enrichment such as hanging vines and leafy branches around the cage. You may also need some basic supplies such as a water bottle to mist the cage to maintain humidity, food bowls, and a wide-toothed comb to brush your sloth's fur. You should aim to spend between $50 and $100 (£45 - £90) on cage accessories.

Lighting – The amount of lighting you need for your sloth cage will vary depending on which species you choose.

Two-toed sloths are nocturnal so they will sleep during the day and become active at night – having bright lighting in the cage could be stressful for these sloths. Three-toed sloths, on the other hand, are active during the day so you might want to set up a lighting system on an automatic timer to ensure that your sloth cage is properly lit throughout the day. You should budget for a lighting cost between $50 and $200 (£45 - £180).

Initial Costs for Sloths	
Type of Cost	**Estimated Cost**
Purchase Price	$1,500 to $3,000 (£1,350 - £2,700)
Cage Materials	$500 to $2,000 (£450 - £1,800)
Cage Accessories	$50 to $100 (£45 - £90)
Lighting System	$50 to $200 (£45 - £180)
Total	$2,100 to $5,300 (£1,890 - £4,770)

*Estimates based on an exchange rate of $1: £0.90. Estimates and rates are subject to change.

b) Monthly Costs

The monthly costs associated with keeping sloths are those that you must cover on a recurring basis. These costs may include the cost of food, bedding, veterinary care, and repairs/replacements for the cage. Below you will find a brief explanation of each cost as well as an estimate and total cost summary.

Food – In the wild, sloths subsist primarily on leaves though they will sometimes eat insects and fruit. In captivity, sloths need to have constant access to vegetation – it is their primary source of nutrition and the only way they get water. There is little information available about the recommended diet for captive sloths but you should plan to provide a mixture of zoological-grade prepared food and fresh fruit and vegetables. Budget a monthly cost of about $50 to $150 (£45 - £135) to feed your sloth.

Bedding – Sloths do not spend much time on the ground – they will only come down from the trees every few days to defecate and urinate. Sloths typically dig a hole to bury their excrement, so the bottom of your sloth cage should be lined with dirt or some kind of soft substrate the sloth can dig into. Lining the bottom of your sloth cage with soil will also help to maintain humidity levels. You will only need to spot-clean the substrate as needed so the cost will not be particularly high. You should budget a cost of $10 to $25 (£9 - £22.50) per month for bedding and substrate.

Veterinary Care – One of the biggest recurring expenses you may have with your sloth is veterinary care. If your sloth gets sick you won't be able to just take him to your local vet – you will need to locate an exotics vet or a zoo vet, and that can get expensive. You should expect to pay a minimum of $50 (£45) for a regular check-up but the visit is more likely to cost $100 (£90) or more – this is just the base price, it does not include the cost of diagnostic testing and treatments. To be on the safe side, budget an annual cost of $240 (£216) for veterinary services – this can be averaged out to about $20 (£18) per month.

Unexpected Costs – In addition to the monthly costs already described you should have a little extra money set aside each month for unexpected costs. These costs may include the cost to make repairs to your sloth cage or replacement of certain supplies. You won't have these costs every month, but you should be prepared just in case by budgeting an extra $20 (£18) for necessities.

Monthly Costs for Sloths	
Type of Cost	**Estimated Cost**
Food	$50 to $150 (£45 - £135)
Bedding	$10 to $25 (£9 - £22.50)
Veterinary Care	$20 (£18)
Unexpected Costs	$20 (£18)
Total	$100 to $215 (£90 - £194)

*Estimates based on an exchange rate of $1: £0.90. Estimates and rates are subject to change.

5) Pros and Cons of the Sloth

Before you decide whether or not the sloth is the right pet for you, you need to take the time to learn everything you can about them – this includes learning the pros and cons of sloths as pets. Below you will find a list of pros and cons to consider regarding sloths as pets.

Sloth Pros

- The sloth is considered a very "cute" pet, popular with young children.
- Sloths are very slow-moving animals so you don't have to worry much about them escaping.
- The sloth is not a noisy animal and it is unlikely to exhibit destructive behavior in the home.
- Sloths are fairly clean animals, coming down from the trees to relieve themselves only once a week or so.
- When properly domesticated, the sloth can be friendly and affectionate.

Sloth Cons

- The sloth is a wild animal (and some species are endangered) so they are very difficult to obtain legally.
- Sloths require a very specialized habitat that allows them to remain in the trees for the most part.
- The sloth has very specialized dietary needs – it feeds almost exclusively on one genus of trees in the wild.
- If you can find a sloth to buy legally it is likely to be extremely expensive.
- The costs to keep a sloth may be prohibitive – in addition to habitat and food you may face high costs for specialty veterinarian visits.
- Many establishments like apartment complexes and condos have rules against keeping exotic pets.
- The sloth lives for an average of 20 to 30 years so it is a long-term commitment.
- Sloths come from a neotropical environment so they need to be kept in a warm, humid enclosure.
- The sloth sleeps for 10 to 15 hours per day and it is nocturnal so it won't be a very active pet.

Chapter Four: Caring for the Sloth

By now you know that the sloth is an arboreal mammal that spends most of its life high up in the trees. The sloth is adapted this kind of habitat and it does not do well on the ground. This being the case, if you plan to keep a sloth you will need to recreate his native habitat in your home. In addition to providing your sloth with plenty of space and branches to climb you also need to maintain proper humidity and temperature levels to keep your sloth healthy. In this chapter you will learn about the habitat needs of sloths and receive tips to recreate it.

1) Habitat Requirements

The most important thing you need to remember when building a habitat for your sloth is the fact that these animals are arboreal – they live in the trees. Your sloth will not be happy (or healthy) if you keep him in a cage that doesn't give him anything to climb. Your sloth needs to be able to climb around on branches and vines because that it how his body is designed – his anatomy doesn't make it easy for him to walk on the ground. In fact, if you leave your sloth on the ground he will be forced to drag himself along using his claws.

The best kind of habitat for a pet sloth is a walk-in style aviary enclosure. The cage should be about 8 feet (244 cm) high and decorated with plenty of branches, vines, ropes, and other structures that the sloth can cling to and climb on. Keep in mind that the sloth spends most of its life hanging upside down from branches (even as it sleeps), so you do not need to worry about providing platforms in the cage – your sloth won't use them.

If you plan to build your own sloth cage, your best bet is to build a metal or wooden frame and then enclose the cage with heavy-gauge wire mesh. Make sure the mesh is strong enough to hold your sloth if he tries to climb on it and the space between the wires should be large enough that your sloth's claws won't get stuck in it. If you have the option, you can build your sloth cage around a tree to provide your sloth with plenty of natural places to climb or you can construct a network of branches and ropes for your sloth to climb on.

In addition to providing your sloth with plenty of space for climbing, you also need to make sure that the temperature and humidity in your sloth cage meets your sloth's requirements. Sloths come from naturally hot and humid environments, so that is the kind of environment you need to cultivate in your sloth cage. The sloth has a relatively low body temperature (compared to other mammals) so keeping it in a warm climate is extremely important. In the sloth's native environment, the temperatures generally remain between 68°F and 93°F (20°C to 34°C), so keep the temperature in your sloth cage within this range.

You should also strive to keep the humidity level in your sloth cage fairly high. You can accomplish this by lining the bottom with soil or some other substrate that will hold moisture. Misting the cage with warm water at least once a day will also help to maintain humidity. Aim for a humidity level between 40% and 60% - you will probably have difficulty maintaining anything higher than that in your home, though if you can reach a higher humidity it will be closer to your sloth's natural environment.

If you don't have the option of building a large cage for your sloth, another acceptable option is setting up a room in your house to keep your sloth. You can control the temperature in the room using a thermostat and you can build structures for climbing using PVC pipe, natural branches, rope, and other materials. You should only keep your sloth in an outdoor cage if you can guarantee a stable temperature within the proper range – this is unlikely unless you live in a tropical location. To give your sloth a place to relieve himself, place a sandbox or similar structure filled with soil somewhere in the room, preferably at the base of a climbing structure so your sloth doesn't have to go far to find it.

2) Accessorizing Your Sloth Cage

The most important accessories for your sloth cage are objects and structures that your sloth can climb on. If you don't have the option of building your sloth cage around a tree then you can still use real branches to create climbing structures – just be sure that the branches you choose come from non-toxic species because your sloth might chew on them. <u>Some of the best species to use for sloths are</u>:

- Alder
- Maple
- Bamboo
- Birch
- Butterfly bush

- Dogwood
- Hazelnut
- Hawthorne
- Beech
- Fennel

- Mint
- Catnip
- Poplar
- Berries

- Willow
- Elm
- Grapes

In addition to branches, you should also decorate your sloth enclosure with thick ropes that he can use to travel from one structure to the next. To ensure your sloth's safety, be sure to anchor your climbing structures securely to the floor of the cage and affix the ropes so that they are fairly taut and so they won't sag under the weight of your sloth. To give your sloth enrichment opportunities, place some vegetable leaves around the enclosure so your sloth has to forage to find them.

3) Sloth Cage Maintenance

The sloth is a fairly clean pet and it only defecates and urinates every few days. This being the case, maintaining sanitary conditions in your sloth cage shouldn't be too difficult. You should take inventory of your sloth cage once a day to make sure that it is clean. When your sloth relieves himself in the substrate you should clean it up as quickly as possible and add new substrate to cover the area. Keep an eye on the surfaces in your sloth cage to make sure that the humidity doesn't facilitate the growth of fungus or mold that could make your sloth sick.

In addition to keeping your sloth cage clean, you also need to monitor things like light and ventilation. The amount of light your sloth needs will vary depending on the species – three-toed sloths are diurnal while two-toed sloths are nocturnal. If you have a nocturnal species you should avoid bright lighting during the day. If you have a diurnal species, you should equip your sloth enclosure to receive about 12 hours of full-spectrum light per day. Ideally, you should put your lighting system on an automatic timer.

In terms of ventilation you want to make sure that your sloth cage doesn't become stagnant – if it is too hot and wet you will end up with mold or fungus which could be dangerous for your sloth's health. At the same time, you want to avoid exposing your sloth to drafts because their body temperature is naturally so low. If you keep your sloth in a room with windows or doors to the outside, make sure they are properly sealed and weather-proofed to prevent any drafts.

Chapter Five: Feeding Your Sloth

One of the main obstacles that stands in the way of people keeping sloths as pets is the fact that they require a very specialized diet. In the wild, sloths have unlimited access to the kinds of food they need but in captivity (especially in areas outside the sloth's native habitat) it can be difficult to acquire these foods. Because many people who keep sloths as pets fail to educate themselves properly about the animals' needs, many sloths in captivity suffer from malnutrition. In this chapter you will find some basic information about the nutritional needs of these lovely animals as well as tips for feeding a captive sloth.

1) Sloth Nutritional Needs

In the wild, sloths follow a highly specialized diet consisting primarily of the tender buds and shoots of trees as well as their leaves. Sometimes the sloth will also eat some fruit, various types of insects, small reptiles, and even small rodents. The diet of the sloth is very low in nutrition and requires special anatomical adaptations to digest. The sloth's digestive system works very slowly to digest high-fiber leaves – it can take up to a month for the sloth's food to be completed digested and absorbed.

To help you get a feel for the natural diet of sloths, consider the following lists of foods sloths have been observed eating in their native habitat:

Leaves

- Almond (*Prunus dulcis*)
- Barrigon leaf buds
- Cecropia trees
- Chocolate bush
- Espave (Anacardium excelsum)
- Jobo (*Spondias* species)
- Liana leaf buds
- Mango (*Mangifera indica*)

Flowers

- Barrigon flowers (*Pseudobombax septenatum*)
- Bombacaceae flowers
- Flowering vines
- Poro Poro (*Cochlospermum vitifolium*)
- Red hibiscus flowers

Fruits

- Almond nuts (*Prunus dulcis*)
- Immature fruit of *Gustavia superba*
- Immature fruit of wild plum (*Spondias* species)
- Fresh mango (*Mangifera indica*)

There is still a great deal to be learned about the ideal diet for sloths in captivity, but most zoos and sloth sanctuaries feed their sloths a combination of fresh vegetables and commercial pellets. Some of the best vegetables to feed your sloth include low-sugar vegetables that are high in fiber – these include things like squash, sweet potato, green beans, carrots, and red peppers. Your sloth with also enjoy leafy vegetables like lettuce, kale, spinach, etc. You can also think about offering your sloth small portions of various fruits like apples, bananas, pears, grapes, berries, mango, avocado, and melon.

To ensure that your sloth's nutritional needs are being met, you might want to supplement his diet of fresh fruits and vegetables with some commercial food. Several manufacturers of exotic pet food offer formulas that are specifically designed for leaf-eating species. You can find leaf eater diets available from companies like Exotic Nutrition, Marion, and Mazuri. Your sloth may or may not actually accept these foods but it is worth offering them to ensure that your sloth receives adequate nutrition.

The Sloth Center feeds their sloths a mixture of commercial high-fiber pellets and fresh fruits and vegetables. <u>In addition, they mix the following supplements into their staple sloth diet</u>:

- ½ teaspoon food-grade diatomaceous earth (for internal parasite control)
- ½ teaspoon of freeze-dried mealworms, crushed
- ½ teaspoon powdered blue-green algae
- ¼ teaspoon Embauba* powder

*Embauba powder is derived from rainforest trees belonging to the Cecropia genus.

2. Sample Diets in Captivity

Unfortunately, there is little information about the proper diet for sloths in captivity so you will have to go through some trial and error to find the right diet for your pet sloth. To help you craft your sloth's diet, consider the diets fed to captive sloths at the Oregon Zoo and the Toronto Zoo. Below you will find an overview of the captive diet fed to Hoffmann's two-toed sloth (*Choloepus hoffmanni*) at the Oregon Zoo and the Toronto Zoo.

Oregon Zoo Daily Diet

- 13g bananas or grapes
- 20g carrots, broccoli or green pepper

- 40g cooked yams or sweet potato
- 60g apples
- 75g leafy greens (spinach, kale or lettuce)
- 100g commercial primate diet
- 7 pieces leaf-eating primate food

Toronto Zoo Daily Diet

- 10g broccoli
- 10g cooked yams or sweet potato
- 15g cantaloupe
- 15g romaine lettuce
- 15g fruit gel
- 15g hardboiled egg
- 25g commercial primate soft gel
- 30g fresh spinach
- 40g avocado
- 40g fresh pears
- 60g bananas
- 200g apples

The diet a captive sloth receives will vary greatly depending where it is kept. Sloths living in rehabilitation centers and rescues (such as the Sloth Sanctuary in Costa Rica) receive a more natural diet because some of the foods they eat in their native habitat are readily available. For sloths kept in other parts of the world, however, these foods are not available so substitutions must be made. Below you will find a list of the kinds of natural foods captive sloths are fed in sloth rescues and rehabilitation centers as well as a list of foods captive sloths receive in zoos and other parts of the world.

Natural Foods for Captive Sloths

- Apples, pears and grapes
- Avocado
- Almond leaves and nuts
- Carrots
- Cayote
- Chocolate bush leaves
- Flowering vines
- Green mangos
- Greens (spinach, kale, lettuce, etc.)
- High-fiber bread
- Hobo leaves (wild plum tree)
- Long green beans
- Mango leaves and ripe fruit
- Popos (red hibiscus flowers)
- Plantains
- Sweet potatoes

Store-Bought Foods for Captive Sloths

<u>Vegetables</u>:

- Broccoli
- Cayote
- Carrot
- Celery
- Escarole
- Green beans
- Green pepper

- Kale
- Lettuce
- Peas
- Spinach
- Sweet potato
- White potato

<u>Fruits</u>:

- Apple
- Avocado
- Banana
- Cantaloupe
- Figs
- Fruit cocktail
- Fruit gel

- Grapes
- Green mango
- Melon
- Orange
- Pears
- Plantains

<u>Protein and Other</u>:

- Canned dog food
- Canned salmon
- Fresh ground smelt
- Fresh white cheese
- Ground horsemeat
- Hardboiled eggs (with shells)

- High-fiber bread
- Leaf eater food (monkey chow)
- Kibbled dog food, moistened
- Pedigree puppy food
- Primate diet, commercial
- Vitamin mineral powder

In addition to these foods, captive sloths are also offered plenty of fresh water. Foods like high-fiber bread and dog food are typically soaked in water as well before feeding because some sloths prefer to take in water through food rather than through drinking.

Chapter Six: Breeding Sloths

Simply keeping a sloth as a pet is a challenge in and of itself, so breeding sloths is not something you should take on without significant forethought and preparation. Researchers are still learning about the breeding habits of wild sloths so there is not a great deal of information out there regarding the breeding of sloths in captivity. Even if you were to decide that you are up to the challenge of breeding sloths, you will have to go through a great deal of trouble to get the right permits. Therefore, the information in this chapter is intended to be general information to help you better understand sloths – it is not intended to be used as instructions for breeding.

1) *Sloth Breeding Info*

In the wild, sloths generally mate between the months of September and November – this correlates with the dry season. Most female sloths only bear one baby each year, though sometimes they go longer than a year between mating because it takes them that long to find a suitable mate. Sloths live to be an average of 20 to 30 years in the wild, longer in captivity. When it comes to sexual maturity, however, sloths do not become sexually mature until they are at least 3 years old. Males usually reach sexual maturity around 3 years of age but females may not until they are four to five years old.

When a female sloth goes into estrus and is ready for mating, she will call to males in the area. Male sloths in the area will be attracted by this call and will seek out the female. Male sloths are polygamous – this means that they will mate with multiple females – and they can be territorial. If more than one male responds to the female's call, the two will hang upside down from a branch and swipe at each other with their claws. The winner of the fight earns the right to mate with the female.

Female sloths only carry one baby at a time and they typically do not mate again until the baby is fully independent. The gestation period for sloths varies from one species to another. For some, the gestation period lasts only 5 or 6 months while others remain pregnant for 11 ½ months. Three-toed sloths have a gestation period at the shorter end of the spectrum while two-toed sloths may be pregnant for the better part of a year. Two-toed sloths usually give birth near the beginning of the dry season while three-toed sloths give birth late into the rainy season. The exception to this is the pale-throated three-toed sloth which tends to mate later than other three-toed species and does not give birth until the beginning of the dry season.

When the baby sloth is born, it is already fairly well developed with open eyes – it also has its fur, claws and teeth. The average birthweight for baby sloths is between 10.5 to 14 ounces (300 to 400 g). Immediately after birth, the baby sloth will crawl onto the mother's stomach and cling there until it is ready to become independent. Baby sloths are usually weaned after about 2 to 4 weeks, though they tend to stay with the mother for much longer. The baby sloth may cling to its mother for as few as 4 months, but it generally remains under the mother's protection for 6 to 11 months.

The male sloth plays no role in caring for the baby sloth – it is entirely the mother's responsibility. In many cases, the female will care for the baby very well, fighting to defend it from potential predators. Sometimes, however, if while the baby is still clinging to the mother, it happens to fall, the female will not come down from the trees after it because it does not want to risk exposure to predators. If the baby survives to independence it may still follow the mother around for another 2 to 3 years. When the two do separate, the mother typically goes off to find a new feeding ground, leaving the territory to her offspring.

Chapter Seven: Keeping Your Sloth Healthy

As you have already learned, the key to keeping a sloth healthy in captivity is to provide an adequate habitat as well as a healthy diet. Even if you do your best to provide these things, however, your sloth is still at risk for developing certain diseases. In this chapter you will learn the basics about which diseases are most likely to affect your sloth and you will receive tips for diagnosis and treating them. You will also receive some tips for preventing illness in your sloth by keeping an eye out for malnutrition and by maintaining sanitary conditions.

1) Common Health Problems

Very little is known about the health problems affecting sloths, particularly sloths kept in captivity. In the wild, sloths play host to a variety of organisms including algae, fungi, and parasites but these organisms do not harm the sloth – the actually benefit the sloth. Because so little is known about the health problems affecting sloths this chapter will be devoted to summarizing cases that have been published in zoo and wildlife medicine journals regarding sloths in the wild and in captivity.

Some of the diseases mentioned in these published cases include the following:

- Addison's Disease (Hypoadrenocorticism)
- Ectoparasites
- Gastrointestinal Parasites
- Respiratory Disease
- Renal Disease
- Salmonella and E. Coli

Addison's Disease (Hypoadrenocorticism)

A study published in the *Journal of Zoo and Wildlife Medicine* in 2015 reported an instance of Addison's Disease in a 22-year-old captive-born female Hoffmann's two-toed sloth (*Choloepus hoffmanni*). This sloth presented with symptoms of respiratory distress in addition to signs of hypotension and severe dehydration. A variety of tests were run including an oral examination, blood tests, and various other tests which resulted in a diagnosis of hypoadrenocorticism, or Addison's Disease.

Addison's Disease is a disorder that affects the endocrine system and it occurs when the adrenal glands do not produce enough of certain hormones like cortisol and aldosterone. The female sloth was treated for this condition but, unfortunately, it did not recover. A necropsy of the deceased sloth revealed additional medical problems including multifocal plaques in the intestines as well as abdominal effusion. Other tests revealed significant adrenal cortical atrophy as well as intra-nuclear mucosal inclusions throughout the gastrointestinal tract.

Source: "Hypoadrenocorticism (Addison's Disease) in a Hoffmann's Two-Toed Sloth." <http://zoowildlifejournal.com/doi/abs/10.1638/2014-0003R2.1>

Ectoparasites and Gastrointestinal Parasites

It is well-known that sloths play host to a wide variety of parasites – these parasites live in the sloth's fur and feed off of the other organisms that can be found there. Aside from these beneficial parasites, however, some sloths have been found with other types of ectoparasites and gastrointestinal parasites, according to a study published in the *Journal of Zoo and Wildlife Medicine* in 2015.

The results of a study of 65 Costa Rican sloths (observed over a 1-year period) revealed that 14 carried gastrointestinal parasites and 6 carried ectoparasites. Of the sloths found to be carrying gastrointestinal parasites, 13 were *Choloepus hoffmani* and one was *Bradypus variegates*. The gastrointestinal parasites found on these sloths were about 71% Coccidia, 21% Cestoda, and 7% Spiruroidea. The ectoparasites discovered on these same two sloth species were primarily *Sarcoptes scabiei* mites and *Amblyomma varium* ticks. These results were taken from fecal samples gathered using Sheather's flotation and sedimentation diagnostic techniques.

Source: "Gastrointestinal Parasites and Ectoparasites of *Bradypus variegates* and *Choloepus hoffmanni* sloths in Captivity from Costa Rica." <http://www.ncbi.nlm.nih.gov/pubmed/19368244 >

Respiratory Disease

A study published in the *Journal of Zoo and Wildlife Medicine* in 2015 reported an instance of respiratory disease in a 2-year-old female Hoffmann's Two-Toed Sloth. The sloth presented with severe inspiratory dyspnea accompanied by significant nasal congestion. It was also observed that the sloth displayed open-mouth breathing and nasal exudate. This sloth was treated with anti-inflammatory medication and broad-spectrum antibiotics but the symptoms persisted, despite dedicated supportive care.

Because medical treatment for the respiratory symptoms did not produce any positive result, the sloth was anesthetized so a tracheal sample could be retrieved via bronchoscopy. The sample revealed Bordetella bronchiseptica cultures, so treatment was developed appropriately. The sloth was treated with a combination of dexamethasone and systemic enroloxacin as well as a nebulization of gentamicin, albuterol and saline. After six weeks of treatment, the sloth recovered fully.

Source: "Respiratory Disease Associated with Bordetella bronchiseptica in a Hoffmann's Two-Toed Sloth." <http://zoowildlifejournal.com/doi/abs/10.1638/2008-0086.1>

Renal Disease

In the June 2014 edition of the *Journal of Zoo and Wildlife Medicine* a case of renal disease was reported in a 13-year-old female two-toed sloth (*Choloepus didactylus*). The sloth presented with a prolonged worsening of azotemia and was euthanized when treatments proved ineffective. Azotemia is a condition characterized by the insufficient or dysfunctional filtering of the blood by the kidneys. This typically leads to abnormally high levels of nitrogen-rich compounds (like creatinine and urea) in the blood.

After the sloth was euthanized, a necropsy was performed to identify the cause of the renal disease. It was found that the sloth had bilaterally shrunken kidneys as well as a large neoplastic mass in the right liver lobe – the sloth also exhibited poor body condition overall. Further tests revealed chronic renal disease in combination with metastatic mineralization as well as a diagnosis of hepatocellular carcinoma. The carcinoma is thought to have been solitary and well-differentiated.

Source: "Chronic Renal Disease in a Captive Two-Toed Sloth with Concurrent Hepatocellular Carcinoma." <http://zoowildlifejournal.com/doi/abs/10.1638/2013-0137R2.1>

Salmonella and E. Coli

According to the results of a study published in the *Journal of Zoo and Wildlife Medicine* in 1999, sloths can be carriers of both *Salmonella enteritidis* and *Escherichia coli* (*E. coli*) bacteria. This study was conducted over a 20-year period on 51 sloth specimens at the Sao Paulo Zoo, 31 of which were *Bradypus sp.* And 17 of which were *Choloepus sp.* This study revealed a total of 81 clinical disorders over the course of the study, including respiratory problems, digestive disorders, nutritional deficiencies, and physical injuries. It was found that more than 96% of the diseases identified occurred within the animal's first 6 months in captivity.

Another study regarding the existence of Salmonella bacteria in sloths was published in the American Journal of Tropical Medicine and Hygiene in 1976. This study covered 974 Panamanian forest animals including various Choloepus species like the sloth. More than 10 serotypes of Salmonella were identified and it was found that the highest incidence of infection occurred during the dry season in Panama which typically lasts from January through April.

Source: "Panamanian Forest Mammals as Carriers of Salmonella." <http://www.ncbi.nlm.nih.gov/pubmed/937635 >

2) *Preventing Illness in Sloths*

No matter how careful you are, you will probably have to deal with a sick sloth at some point. Because it is difficult to find a veterinarian who is trained to treat sloths you want to find a vet for your sloth before he actually needs one. This way, you can contact the vet quickly as soon as your sloth becomes ill so he can receive prompt treatment. You may not be able to completely prevent your sloth from getting sick but you can reduce the risk by making sure your sloth's nutritional needs are being met and by keeping his cage as clean as possible.

a) Dealing with Nutritional Deficiencies

Because it can be difficult to meet the sloth's specialized nutritional needs, nutritional deficiencies in captive sloths are a very real threat. The most important thing you can do to avoid nutritional deficiencies is to learn as much as you can about the sloth's diet and to structure your feeding program around those needs as much as possible. You may not be able to find the exact types of vegetation your sloth would eat in the wild, but you can provide a mixture of different vegetables and supplements to ensure well-rounded nutrition – see the information in Chapter 5 for tips on feeding your sloth.

As careful as you may be about providing for your sloth's nutritional needs, you cannot force your sloth to eat and there is always a risk for nutritional deficiencies. To make sure you catch these problems before they become too advanced you need to learn to identify the symptoms of nutritional deficiencies so you can seek veterinary care for your sloth. One of the most recognizable signs of nutritional deficiency in sloths is impaired motor function. Limb deformations are often caused by calcium deprivation – paralysis and constipation can be signs of vitamin B deficiency. In older sloths, hair loss and dry skin often point to vitamin deficiencies as well as improper levels of omega fatty acids in the diet.

b) Maintaining Sanitary Conditions

Another important aspect of keeping your sloth happy and healthy is maintaining sanitary conditions in your sloth cage. The style and set-up of your cage will have a significant impact on how difficult or easy it is to clean, so consider this when planning out and building your sloth cage. Remember, sloths come down from the trees to relieve themselves and they typically bury their excrement in the dirt. So, plan to keep at least one sizable area of soil substrate in your sloth cage for this purpose. You'll only need to clean the area once a week or so when your sloth relieves himself.

In addition to cleaning out your sloth's litter box, so to speak, you need to keep the rest of the cage clean as well. Sloths have poor vision and hearing, so their sense of smell is their strongest asset. This being the case, you want to avoid cleaning too much of the cage at once because, in doing so, you will be removing the sloth's scent and that could lead to stress or confusion. Try to clean one area of the cage at a time in a continuous rotation to keep things clean without stressing your sloth out.

3) Medical Benefits of Fungus in Sloth Fur

As you have already learned, the sloth's fur exhibits several specialized functions. Not only does it grow in the opposite direction of most mammals' fur, but it also plays host to a variety of microorganisms. The sloth's fur is home to two types of symbiotic algae which help to provide camouflage for the sloth and which serve as food for other microorganisms living in the sloth's fur. The sloth's coat has two layers – the inner layer is short and fine, serving the purpose of keeping the sloth warm. The outer layer is coarse and that is where the algae, fungi, and various parasites live.

According to a study conducted by the Smithsonian Tropical Research Institute and published in PLOS One, some of the fungi found in sloth fur may have disease-fighting implications. During the study, researchers collected samples from nine different sloths living in Soberania National Park in Panama and 84 species of fungus were identified. Of those 84 species, 74 were cultured and three strains of fungus were found to be effective against the MCF-7 strain of breast cancer in humans. This is the most commonly used strain of breast cancer for biomedical research and it is also one of the longest-lived strains.

In addition the fungi species found to be effective against breast cancer, eight showed significant levels of bioactivity against the parasite linked to Chagas disease, *Trypoanosoma cruzi*. Chagas disease is transmitted by insects and it can cause swelling, diarrhea, fever, and enlargement of the liver. Two strains of fungi were effective against the parasite connected to malaria, *Plasmodium falciparum*, and three were shown to be active against both the MCF-7 strain of breast cancer and the *Trypoanosoma cruzi* parasite. It was also found that one species of bacteria living in sloth fur was effective against the methicillin-resistant strain of *Staphylococcus aureus* (MRSA) which kills thousands of people every year.

Chapter Eight: Sloth Care Sheet

Throughout this book you have received a wealth of useful information about the different species of sloths ranging from their habitat, anatomy and behavior to breeding, feeding, and more. Though this book is designed to provide you with a rounded education about these exotic pets, there may come a time when you have additional questions. Rather than flipping through the entire book to find them, use this sloth care sheet to reference specific facts regarding the sloth in general as well as information about its habitat, feeding and breeding.

1) Basic Information

Taxonomy: order Pilosa; family Megalonychidae or Bradypodidae

Species: six species currently identified

Distribution: Central and South America

Habitat: almost entirely arboreal

Size: varies by species, generally 19 to 27 inches (50 to 70cm) long; weigh between 17.5 and 18.75 lbs. (about 8kg)

Body Shape: long arms and legs; short head with large eyes, short snouts and tiny ears; stubby tails; long, curved claws; long tongues

Fur Length: longer in two-toed sloths

Tail: absent in two-toed sloths; 2.4 to 2.75 inches (6 to 7cm) in three-toed sloths

Coloration: varies from one species to another; primarily shades of brown and tan; camouflaged with algae growth

Movement: primarily suspension-based and quadrupedal; very slow and deliberate

Defense Mechanisms: slow movement (doesn't disturb surrounding vegetation); long, sharp claws

Diet: folivore; primarily feeds on tender shoots, buds, and leaves; occasionally eat insects, small reptiles, and birds

Adaptations: multi-compartment stomach filled with symbiotic bacteria; bacteria helps to break down leaves

Metabolism: very slow metabolic rate, half the rate of similar-sized mammals; body temperature as low as 86°F to 93°F (30°C to 34°C) while active

Gestation Period: about 6 to 11 months, varies by species

Infants: born upside down; cling to mother's fur for several weeks then may continue to follow her for up to 4 years

Lifespan: average 20 to 30 years in the wild, often longer in captivity

2) Habitat Set-up Guide

Basic Habitat Requirements: space, temperature, humidity, lighting, ventilation

Space: about 8 feet high; bigger is better

Temperature: between 68°F and 93°F (20°C to 34°C)

Humidity: between 40% and 60%, higher if possible

Lighting: 12 hours of full-spectrum lighting per day; lights on dimmer to simulate dusk and dawn

Indoor vs. Outdoors: only outdoors in proper temperature range; must have access to indoors in cold weather

Cage Materials: sturdy frame of wood, metal or PVC; enclose with heavy-gauge wire mesh

Climbing Structures: branches from non-toxic trees and thick rope; can also use PVC

Cleaning: remove and replace substrate weekly; clean sections of the cage in rotating intervals

3) Nutritional Needs

Diet Type: omnivorous; primarily folivorous

Plant Matter: tender shoots and buds, leaves

Low-Sugar Vegetables: sweet potato, squash, carrots, green beans, red peppers

Leafy Greens: romaine lettuce, green leaf lettuce, kale, spinach, etc.

Fruit: apples, bananas, pears, grapes, berries, and melon

Other: commercial leaf eater diet may be offered

Water: obtained from vegetables and leaves

Supplements: diatomaceous earth, freeze-dried mealworms, powdered glue-green algae, embauba powder

4) Breeding Information

Reproductive Behavior: polygamous

Breeding Frequency: once a year or less

Breeding Season: between September and November

Sexual Maturity (female): 4 to 5 years

Sexual Maturity (male): around 3 years

Estrus Cycle: any time of year; female makes loud calls to attract a mate

Gestation Period: varies by species; 5 to 6 months (two-toed sloth), up to 11.5 months (three-toed sloth)

Giving Birth: beginning of dry season (two-toed species); end of rainy season (three-toed species)

Gap Between Litters: at least 12 months; not until offspring has become independent

Litter Size: one

Sloth Offspring: birthweight 300 to 400 g; placental; born fully developed with open eyes, fur, and claws

Offspring Dependency: clings to mother's belly for 4 to 11 months on average

Nursing: about 2 to 4 weeks until weaned

Independence: weaned within 4 weeks but clings to mother for at least 4 months; may still follow mother around after becoming independent

Sexual Dimorphism: varies by species; females are often larger than males, few other differentiations

Chapter Nine: Relevant Websites

In reading this book you have received a wealth of information about the sloth in general as well as specific tips to care for your sloth. Even after reading this book, however, you may find that you need more information about a certain subject – that is where this chapter comes in. Here you will find links to helpful websites and online resources where you can find additional information about sloths and sloth conservation. You will also find resources for various supplies including food for your sloth as well as cages and cage accessories.

1) Food for Your Sloth

Below you will find a collection of websites about feeding your sloth as well as some resources to help you find sloth food:

Leaf Eating Primate Food. Mazuri.
<http://www.mazuri.com/leafeatingprimates.aspx>

Marion Leaf Eater Food.
<http://www.marionzoological.com/documents/brochures/ MZ-LeafEater-Broch_0814.pdf>

Leaf Eater Diet. Exotic Nutrition.
<http://www.exoticnutrition.com/leafetr.html>

Leaf Eater Diet. PetWiser.com. < http://petwiser.com/Leaf-Eater-Diet-5lbs_p_21.html >

Embauba Powder. Rain-Tree.com. <http://www.rain-tree.com/embauba-powder.htm#.VmtI6_mrQuU >

2) Cages and Cage Supplies for Sloth

Below you will find a collection of websites about housing your sloth as well as resources to help you find cage materials and accessories:

"Walk-In Bird Aviary." Instructables.
<http://www.instructables.com/id/Walk-in-Bird-Aviary/>

Indoor and Outdoor Aviaries. Cages By Design.
<http://www.cagesbydesign.com/t-suncatcherbird.aspx>

Centurion Cage Co. and Centurion Aviaries.
<http://www.centurionaviaries.com/Walkins.html>

Walk-In Aviary Bird Cage. Bird Cages 4 Less.
http://birdcages4less.com/page/B/PROD/Aviaries/PA5659

Wood Tree Stands. Wayfair.com.
<http://www.wayfair.com/Playstands-C530128.html?redir=bird+play+stand&rtype=6&dept=7&ust =>

Wood Floor Bird Stands. Perch Factory.
<http://www.perchfactory.com/bird_floor_stands/wood_flo
or_bird_stands.htm>

Bird Perches, Toys. Safe & Harmful Wood Perch.
<http://www.mdvaden.com/bird_page.shtml

Natural Wood Perches. Perch Factory.
<http://www.perchfactory.com/bird_cage_perches/natural_
wood_perches.htm >

3) Sloth Species Information

Below you will find a collection of websites about the different sloth species so you can learn more about these unique animals:

"Hoffmann's Two-Toed Sloth." The Animal Files.
<http://www.theanimalfiles.com/mammals/anteaters_relati ves/hoffmanns_two_toed_sloth.html >

"Sloth Facts: Habits, Habitat & Diet." Live Science.
<http://www.livescience.com/27612-sloths.html>

"Three-Toed Sloth." National Geographic.
<http://animals.nationalgeographic.com/animals/mammals/ three-toed-sloth/>

"The Species of Sloth." Mom.me Animals.
<http://animals.mom.me/species-sloth-4919.html>

"Sloth Fact Sheet." World Animal Foundation.
<http://www.worldanimalfoundation.net/f/sloth.pdf>

"Sloths – Facts, Diet and Habitat Information." Animal Corner. <https://animalcorner.co.uk/animals/sloth/>

"Sloth Species." World Wildlife Fund. <http://www.worldwildlife.org/species/sloth >

4) Conservation Information for Sloths

Below you will find a collection of websites about sloth conservation as well as links to various sloth rescue organizations that you can donate to:

Sloth Sanctuary of Costa Rica – Support the Sloths.
<http://www.slothsanctuary.com/donate-to-support-the-sloth-sanctuary/>

World Wildlife Fund – How to Help.
<http://www.worldwildlife.org/how-to-help>

The Sloth Institute Costa Rica – How You Can Help.
<http://www.theslothinstitutecostarica.org/how-you-can-help/>

Costa Rica Animal Rescue Center – Volunteer.
<http://www.costaricaanimalrescuecenter.org/volunteer/>

AIUNAU Organization – Donate.
<http://www.aiunau.org/en/#search-2>

Chapter Ten: Frequently Asked Questions

Sloths are beautiful and interesting creatures which is part of what makes them popular as an exotic pet. Reading this book should not only answer most your questions about sloths in general, but also about keeping them as pets. Because there is so much to learn about sloths, however, you may find that you still have questions after working through this book. In this chapter you will find a collection of frequently asked questions about sloths to help you supplement your new-found knowledge about these wonderful animals.

Q: *Why are sloths popular as exotic pets?*

A: Sloths are amazing and beautiful creatures, but that is just a small part of what makes them popular as exotic pets. Many people like sloths because they have seen videos of "cute" sloths online and they have heard that sloths are affectionate pets. Compared to traditional pets like cats and dogs, sloths are unique and interesting but they can also be challenging to keep. Sloths move very slowly so there is little risk of them escaping and they are very clean, only urinating or defecating about once per week.

Q: *How many different types of sloth are there?*

A: There are six different species of sloth divided between two taxonomical families – Megalonychidae and Bradypodidae. Five of the six species are individual, but the Hoffmann's Two-Toed Sloth (Choloepus hoffmanni) has five additional subspecies.

Q: *What is the difference between two-toed and three-toed sloths?*

A: There are a number of important differences between two-toed and three-toed sloths. For one thing, two-toed sloths only have two clawed fingers on their front limbs while three-toed sloths have three – both types have three clawed toes on their hind limbs. Another difference is that two-toed sloths are a little larger than three-toed sloths and they are nocturnal rather than diurnal.

Q: *Why is it difficult to keep a sloth as a pet?*

A: For one thing, it is very difficult to obtain a sloth legally because it is a wild animal. Some states in the United States do not have restrictions on keeping wild animals as pets, but you will still find it challenging to obtain a sloth legally. In addition to the difficulty of finding a sloth, keeping sloths healthy in captivity is a challenge. Sloths have very specialized diets and they are very prone to nutritional deficiencies. If your sloth gets sick, you won't be able to take him to a regular veterinarian for treatment – you'll have to find an exotics vet or a zoo vet.

Q: *Can I breed my pet sloth?*

A: Unfortunately there is little information available about the breeding habits of sloths because observation of sloths in the wild is very difficult. Breeding sloths is challenging for a number of reasons. For one thing, it is hard to tell the difference between male and female sloths. Additionally, it is difficult enough to obtain one sloth legally, so finding and purchasing two sloths for breeding will be even more of a challenge for you. If you do manage to find two sloths and breed them, caring for the baby can be difficult as well.

Q: *Why do sloths move so slowly?*

A: If you know anything about sloths, you probably know that they are some of the slowest-moving mammals in the world. There are several different factors that contribute to the slow motion of these animals. For one thing, the slower the sloth moves, the less likely it is to be spotted by a predator. Second, the sloth's natural diet is very low in nutrients and energy so the sloth doesn't have a great deal of energy to expend on motion.

Q: *What is the life cycle of the sloth like in the wild?*

A: Two-toed sloths have a gestation period of 6 to 12 months while three-toed sloths have a shorter gestation period lasting about 5 to 6 months. Both types of sloth generally mate once a year and they only birth one baby at a time. Baby sloths are weaned after a few weeks but they generally continue to follow the mother around for at least a year, often clinging to her fur for 9 to 12 months. Male sloths reach sexual maturity around 3 years while females take 4 to 5 years to mature. The average lifespan of a sloth in the wild is 20 to 30 years.

Q: *How do sloths get around in the wild?*

A: The sloth is adapted to life in the trees – it possesses long, curved claws on the end of each toe that it uses to cling to branches, moving along upside down. Sloths do come down to the ground about once a week or so to relieve themselves but they have a hard time moving on the ground. Although sloths are very slow on the ground and in the trees, they are very good swimmers.

Q: *Do sloths live in groups in the wild?*

A: Though research is still being conducted, it is thought that sloths are largely a solitary species in the wild. Male sloths are very territorial and will defend their territory against other males by fighting with their sharp claws. Female sloths will share their territory with their young for as long as 3 to 4 years, then they will move to a new territory, leaving the existing territory to their young.

Index

A

accessories   40, 41, 52, 88, 90

adaptations   4, 7, 57

Addison's Disease   70, 71

algae   8, 13, 14, 20, 22, 59, 70, 79, 82, 85

anatomy   81

ancestors   30

anteaters   7, 29, 92

arboreal   3, 7, 12, 14, 24, 25, 29, 30, 41, 48, 49, 82

armadillos   29

arms   13, 82

B

baby   4, 12, 38, 66, 67

bacteria   10, 13, 14, 20, 75, 80, 83

bedding   43, 44

behavior   81

birth   12, 67

birthweight   67, 86

black market   34

blood tests   71

Bradypodidae   7, 29

branches   1, 10, 22, 41, 48, 49, 50, 51, 52, 53, 84

breeding   11, 65, 81

Brown-Throated Sloth   16, 19

budget   41, 42, 44

buds   7, 13, 57, 82, 85

buy   41, 47

C

cage   40, 41, 43, 44, 49, 50, 51, 52, 53, 54, 76, 78, 84, 88, 90, 91
calcium   77
camouflage   8, 79
canopy   1, 7, 22, 26
captivity   4, 2, 13, 43, 56, 58, 60, 65, 66, 69, 70, 75, 83
care   4, 1, 2, 31, 32, 40, 44, 67, 73, 77, 81, 88, 112
care sheet   81
Cecropia   7, 24, 57, 59
children   46
CITES   3, 35, 37
claws   1, 7, 10, 11, 13, 17, 22, 31, 49, 50, 66, 67, 82, 86
clean   43, 46, 54, 76, 78, 84
climate   21, 50
color   17, 18, 20, 21
conception   3
conditions   54, 69, 78
conservation   4, 5, 2, 15, 94
convergent evolution   29
cost   40, 43
costs   33, 40, 43, 44, 47

D

defecate   11, 43
defense mechanism   11
deforestation   14
dehydration   71
dentition   9
destructive behavior   46
diagnosis   69, 71, 74
diet   2, 69, 77
digest   4, 10, 21, 24, 57

distress 71

diurnal 22, 54

dry season 21, 66, 67, 75, 86

E

E. Coli 70, 75

ears 13, 17, 20, 82

ecosystem 8, 14

Ectoparasites 70, 72

enclosure 39, 41, 47, 49, 53, 54

endangered 3, 35, 36, 37

energy 9, 10, 11

enrichment 41, 53

evolution 5, 30

excrement 43, 78

exotic pet 1, 59

extinct 1, 30

F

facts 4, 2, 81

feeding 4, 56, 64, 68, 77, 81, 89

feet 13, 82

female 3, 12, 66, 67, 71, 73, 74, 86

fiber 57, 58, 59, 62, 63, 64

fingers 25, 29

food 4, 7, 9, 13, 39, 41, 43, 47, 56, 57, 59, 61, 63, 64, 79, 83, 88, 89

forage 53

forest 4, 5, 21, 29, 75

fruit 39, 43, 57, 58, 61, 62

fungus 54, 79

fur 8, 9, 12, 13, 14, 18, 20, 24, 26, 28, 38, 41, 67, 72, 79, 80, 83, 86, 112

G

gastrointestinal	71, 72
gestation period	67

H

habitat	2, 14, 31, 39, 46, 47, 48, 49, 56, 57, 61, 69, 81
head	13, 17, 20, 24, 82
health problems	70
healthy	2, 69
hearing	12, 78
herbivore	4
history	4
Hoffman's Two-Toed Sloth	16, 25, 112
humidity	41, 43, 48, 50, 54, 84

I

illegal	36, 37
initial cost	40
injury	3, 31
insects	7, 8, 13, 14, 20, 22, 43, 57, 80, 82, 83
IUCN	2, 14

L

leaves	4, 7, 10, 13, 24, 28, 43, 53, 57, 62, 82, 85
legal	34, 36
length	17, 19, 23, 26, 27
licensing	33, 34
lifespan	12
lighting	40, 41, 54, 84

| limbs | 9, 17, 25, 27, 29 |
| Linnaeus' Two-Toed Sloth | 16, 27 |

M

male	3, 12, 22, 38, 66, 67, 86, 108
malnutrition	56, 69
mammal	1, 7, 29, 48
mane	22
Maned Sloth	14, 16, 21
mangroves	24
mate	12, 66, 86
materials	90
Megalonychidae	7, 12, 29, 82
metabolic rate	10, 13, 83
metabolism	10
microorganisms	79
mold	54
monthly costs	43
movement	7, 8, 10, 13, 82

N

native	1, 14, 48, 50, 56, 57, 61
necropsy	71, 74
night	4
nocturnal	25, 28, 42, 47, 54
noise	11
nose	17, 20
nutrients	10
nutrition	24, 43, 57, 59, 77
nutritional needs	31, 56, 59, 76, 77
Nycticebus	12, 82

O

omnivore   4

P

Pale-Throated Sloth   16, 17
Parasites   70, 72
permit   34, 36, 37
pet   4, 2, 36, 46
Pilosa   7, 12, 29, 82
plant   4
poaching   14
polygamous   66, 86
predator   8, 11
predators   3
pregnant   67
prevent   36, 55, 76
price   40, 41, 44
pros and cons   2, 46
protection   35, 67
purchase   12, 37, 40, 41
Pygmy Three-Toed Sloth   14, 16, 23

R

rehabilitation   61
Renal Disease   70, 74
repairs   43
requirements   34
rescue   36, 37, 94
research   31, 35, 79
resources   88, 89, 90

S

Salmonella 70, 75
sanitary 54, 69, 78
sexual dimorphism 12
sexual maturity 12, 66
size 5, 9, 10, 19, 22, 24, 25, 26, 41
sloth4, 5, 1, 2, 4, 7, 8, 9, 10, 11, 12, 14, 15, 16, 17, 18, 19, 20, 21, 22, 23, 24, 25, 26, 27, 28, 29, 30, 31, 33, 34, 35, 36, 37, 38, 39, 40, 41, 43, 44, 46, 47, 48, 49, 50, 51, 52, 53, 54, 56, 57, 58, 59, 60, 61, 65, 66, 67, 69, 70, 71, 72, 73, 74, 75, 76,77, 78, 79, 80, 81, 86, 88, 89, 90, 92, 93, 94, 108, 109, 110, 112, 113, 114
Sloth Sanctuary 14, 15, 61, 94, 113
smell 11, 78
social 38, 39
social structure 38
South America 1, 12, 17, 19, 25, 27, 29, 82
species 1, 2, 3, 5, 6, 7, 8, 9, 12, 13, 14, 15, 16, 17, 18, 19, 20, 21, 23, 24, 25, 26, 27, 28, 29, 30, 31, 34, 35, 36, 37, 39, 41, 46, 52, 54, 57, 58, 59, 67, 72, 75, 79, 80, 81, 82, 83, 86, 87, 92, 93, 113
speed 10
spine 9
stomach 10, 13, 67, 83
subspecies 26
substrate 14, 43, 50, 54, 78, 84
supplies 41, 44, 88
symbiotic 8, 10, 13, 20, 79, 83
symptoms 71, 73, 77

T

tail 9, 13, 17, 19, 22, 24, 26, 27, 82

teeth   9, 24, 28, 67

temperature   10, 13, 48, 50, 51, 55, 83, 84

territorial   66

testing   44

three-toed   2, 7, 9, 13, 17, 19, 20, 21, 23, 24, 25, 26, 27, 29, 30, 54, 67, 82, 86, 92, 108, 114

timer   42, 54

tips   2, 33, 34, 48, 56, 69, 77, 88

toes   9, 25, 29

toys   41

trade   3, 37

treatment   32, 73, 76

two-toed   2, 4, 7, 9, 13, 20, 25, 26, 27, 28, 29, 30, 54, 60, 67, 71, 74, 82, 86, 114

U

urinate   11, 43

V

vegetables   43, 58, 59, 77, 85

vegetation   7, 10, 13, 14, 21, 43, 77, 82

vertebrae   9

vet   32, 44, 76

veterinarian   32, 47, 76

veterinary care   43

vines   41, 49, 58, 62

W

water   10, 28, 41, 43, 50, 64

weaned   13, 38, 67, 83, 86, 87

websites   3, 88, 89, 90, 92, 94
weight   18, 53
wild   4, 35, 37, 38, 39
World Wildlife Fund   14, 15, 93, 94, 113

Z

zoo   32, 36, 39, 44, 70

Photo Credits

Cover Photo By Stefan Laube via Wikimedia Commons, <https://en.wikipedia.org/wiki/File:Bradypus.jpg>

Page 1 Photo by Christian Mehlfuhrer via Wikimedia Commons, <https://en.wikipedia.org/wiki/File:MC_Drei-Finger-Faultier.jpg>

Page 6 Photo By Masteraah via Wikimedia Commons, <https://en.wikipedia.org/wiki/File:Sloth1a.jpg>

Page 17 Photo By Fernando Flores via Wikimedia Commons, <https://en.wikipedia.org/wiki/File:Bradypus_tridactylus_-Parque_del_Este,_Caracas,_Venezuela-8.jpg>

Page 19 Photo By D. Gordon E. Robertson via Wikimedia Commons, <https://en.wikipedia.org/wiki/File:Brown-throated_three-toed_sloth_male.jpg>

Page 21 Photo By Paulo B. Chaves via Wikimedia Commons, <https://en.wikipedia.org/wiki/File:B_torquatus_Paulo_Chaves.jpg>

Page 23 Photo By C. Horwitz via Wikimedia Commons, <https://en.wikipedia.org/wiki/File:Baby_Choloepus_hoffm anni,_Costa_Rica.JPG>

Page 25 Photo By Geoff Gallice via Wikimedia Commons, <https://en.wikipedia.org/wiki/File:Choloepus_hoffmanni_(Puerto_Viejo,_CR)_crop.jpg>

Page 27 Photo By Dave Pape via Wikimedia Commons, <https://en.wikipedia.org/wiki/File:Choloepus_didactylus_2 _-_Buffalo_Zoo.jpg>

Page 33 Photo By Tony Hisgett via Wikimedia Commons, <https://commons.wikimedia.org/wiki/File:Two_toed_Sloth _6_(4871961869).jpg>

Page 48 Photo By Jsfouche via Wikimedia Commons, https://commons.wikimedia.org/wiki/File:2_toed_sloth.jpg

Page 52 Photo By Flickr user Marinakvillatoro, <https://www.flickr.com/photos/lifeoftravel/3369221544/siz es/o/>

Page 56 Photo By Fruitwerks via Wikimedia Commons, <https://en.wikipedia.org/wiki/File:Three-toed_Tree_Sloth_enjoying_a_snack_(frontal_view).jpg>

Page 60 Photo By Stevenj via Wikimedia Commons, <https://en.wikipedia.org/wiki/File:Two-toed_sloth_Costa_Rica_-_cropped.jpg>

Page 65 Photo By Ontley via Wikimedia Commons, <https://commons.wikimedia.org/wiki/File:Two_toed_sloth.JPG>

Page 69 Photo By Flickr user Marissa_strniste, <https://www.flickr.com/photos/mstrniste/6854263759/sizes/l>

Page 76 Photo By Flickr user Praziquentel, <https://www.flickr.com/photos/praziquantel/30950009/sizes/l>

Page 81 Photo By Dave Pape via Wikimedia Commons, <https://en.wikipedia.org/wiki/File:Choloepus_didactylus_-_Buffalo_Zoo.jpg>

Page 88 Photo By Sergiodelgado via Wikimedia Commons,
<https://en.wikipedia.org/wiki/File:SlothDWA.jpg>

Page 95 Photo By D. Gordon E. Robertson,
<https://en.wikipedia.org/wiki/File:Hoffman%27s_Two-
toed_Sloth,_Monteverde.jpg

References

"A Guide to Sloth Pet Care." HubPages. <http://hubpages.com/animals/pet-sloth-care>

"Appendices I, II and III." CITES.org. <https://cites.org/eng/app/appendices.php>

"Are Sloths Good Pets?" LovetoKnow. < http://small-pets.lovetoknow.com/choosing-small-pet/are-sloths-good-pets>

"Behavioral Studies and Rehabilitation of Sloths in *Parque Natural Metropolitano*." Smithsonian Tropical Research Institute. <https://www.mcgill.ca/files/pfss/Sloths_Report.pdf>

"Can You Keep a Sloth as a Pet?" Buzzle.com. <http://www.buzzle.com/articles/can-you-keep-a-sloth-as-a-pet.html>

"Fungi in Sloth Fur Could Have a Wide Variety of Disease-Fighting Implications." IFL Science. <http://www.iflscience.com/health-and-medicine/fungi-sloth-fur-could-have-wide-variety-disease-fighting-implications>

"Hoffman's Two-Toed Sloth." Mac Como Zoo. <http://www.macalester.edu/~montgomery/TwoToedSloth.html>

"How Much Does a Sloth Cost?" HowMuchIsIt.org. <http://www.howmuchisit.org/how-much-does-a-sloth-cost/>

"Reproduction Sloth Style." BioWeb. <http://bioweb.uwlax.edu/bio203/s2008/thomas_joe/reproduction.htm>

"Sloth." World Wildlife Fund. <http://www.worldwildlife.org/species/sloth>

"Sloth Facts: Habits, Habitat & Diet." LiveScience. <http://www.livescience.com/27612-sloths.html>

"Sloth Reproduction." Earj's Ecosystem. <http://earjecosystem.weebly.com/sloth-reproduction.html>

"Sloth Sanctuary – About Us." Sloth Sanctuary Costa Rica. <http://www.slothsanctuary.com/about-us/>

"Sloths: Chew Your Food Slowly." Ceiba.org. <http://www.ceiba.org/articles/sloth.htm>

"Sloths as Pets? Come On!" Born Free USA Blog. <http://www.bornfreeusa.org/bfusablog.php?p=3841&more=1>

"The CITES Appendices." CITES.org.
 <https://www.cites.org/eng/app/index.php>

"Three-Toed Sloth." National Geographic.
 <http://animals.nationalgeographic.com/animm
 als/three-toed-sloth/>

"Two-Toed Sloth." National Aviary.
 <http://www.aviary.org/animals/two-toed-sloth>

"What are the Pros and Cons of Keeping a Pet Sloth?"
 WiseGeek. <http://www.wisegeek.org/what-are-the-
 pros-and-cons-of-keeping-a-pet-sloth.htm>

"What States Allow Ownership of Exotic Animals?"
 Governing.com.
 <http://www.governing.com/news/state/
 Where-Can-You-Own-Exotic-Animals.html>

"Your Weird Animal Questions Answered: Is a Sloth a
 Good Pet?" National Geographic.
 <http://voices.nationalgeographic.com/2014/03/26/pets-
 weird-animal-questions-dogs-sloths-otters-animals-
 science/>